Design: Art of Design
Recipe Photography: Peter Barry
Jacket and Illustration Artwork: Jane Winton, courtesy
of Bernard Thornton Artists, London
Editors: Jillian Stewart and Kate Cranshaw

CHARTWELL BOOKS
A division of Book Sales, Inc.
POST OFFICE BOX 7100
114 Northfield Avenue
Edison, N.J. 08818-7100

CLB 3530
© 1995 CLB Publishing,
Godalming, Surrey, England.
Printed and bound in Singapore
All rights reserved
ISBN 0-7858-0232-0

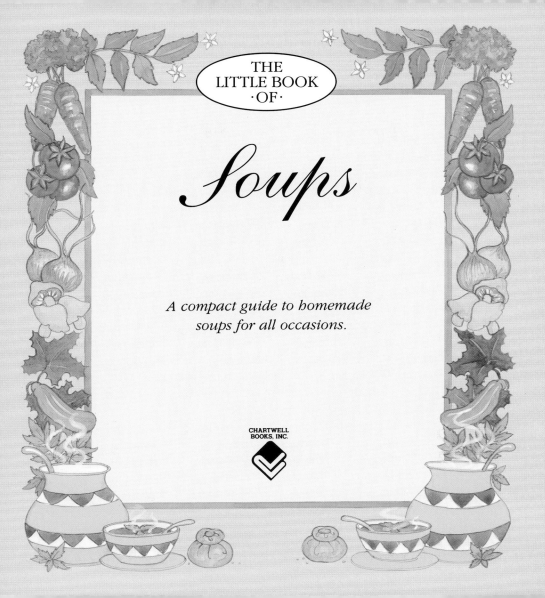

THE
LITTLE BOOK
·OF·

Soups

*A compact guide to homemade
soups for all occasions.*

CHARTWELL
BOOKS, INC.

Introduction

Every country has soups included in its cuisine. Some Western specialty soups are only served in the smartest of establishments; others, particularly in the Far East, are served from roadside stalls from huge bubbling cauldrons. Both will be freshly made and both will probably be equally delicious.

Soups have a very wide appeal, and are enjoyed from infancy right into old age. They vary in consistency from the thinnest consommé to rich and hearty meal-in-one soups. Most soups are served steaming hot, but some can be sipped refreshingly chilled – perfect on a summer's day. Soups serve many occasions. They can be just the thing when you are short of time and need a quick meal, and they can make a delightful start to a meal when you want to linger with friends over several courses.

For all their tremendous variety, soups fall into two main categories. The first is the lighter type, which should stimulate the appetite for the main course without being too filling. The second, perhaps served with good bread and cheese, can make a quick and basic family meal in itself.

Broths form the basis of many soups. These can be based either on meat, vegetables or fish, and are themselves very satisfying to make. The boiling up of a handful of vegetables, a chicken carcass or ham bone, and the addition of a few bay leaves and peppercorns is very easy and will give the finished

soup a rounded, subtle flavor. The boiling of bones can be time-consuming, but with a pressure cooker it only takes 20 minutes. For convenience, the broth may be frozen for later use. And if making your own broth is inconvenient, then bouillon cubes are a tasty and convenient alternative.

Fine ingredients, such as fresh vegetables and herbs, a little wine or sherry, or some interesting spice such as ground coriander, make all the difference to quality when making soups.

Garnishes can alter the appearance of a soup. The aim should be to garnish soups with bright, contrasting colors and complementary flavors. Parsley is always popular for its vivid color and fresh taste. Green onions and chives can be very successful substitutes for parsley, especially to give a welcome lift to the more bland creamy soups. Fresh basil is excellent in tomato-based soups, while grated Parmesan is delicious in moderation on thick, brown soups. A swirl of fresh or sour cream adds panache to the thicker pureed soups and looks more stylish still when topped with a sprinkling of fresh herbs or a spice such as paprika, cayenne, nutmeg or pepper.

Experiment with the appetizing recipes in this book. Some are old favorites, while others are a little unusual – all are delicious and are sure to please both family and friends.

Dumpling Soup

SERVES 6-8

For this Polish soup, the number of dumplings can be increased to serve as a more filling meal, if wished.

PREPARATION: 25 mins
COOKING: 10 mins

1.5 litres/3 pints real beef broth

Filling
6 ounces lean ground beef or pork
1 tsp chopped fresh marjoram
1 small onion, minced or very finely chopped
Salt and pepper

Dough
2 cups all-purpose flour, sifted
Pinch salt
1-2 eggs
4 tbsps water

Chopped parsley

---

1. Combine all the filling ingredients, mixing very well.

2. Prepare the dough by sifting the flour and salt into a large bowl. Make a well in the center, and add the eggs and water. Use only one egg if they are large.

3. Using a wooden spoon, beat the ingredients together, gradually incorporating flour until the

Step 6 Press the edges together to seal well and crimp with a fork.

dough becomes too stiff to beat.

4. Knead the dough until firm but elastic, then roll it out very thinly on a floured surface and cut into 3-inch rounds

5. Place a small spoonful of filling on each circle, and brush the edges with water.

6. Press the edges together to seal well, and crimp with a fork.

7. Bring the broth to the boil and add the dumplings. Cook about 10 minutes, or until all have floated to the surface.

8. Add some chopped parsley to the soup, adjust the seasoning and serve in individual bowls or from a large tureen.

French Onion Soup

SERVES 4

This soup tastes best if cooked the day before it is needed and then reheated as required.

PREPARATION: 10 mins
COOKING: 30 mins

---

3 medium onions
4 tbsps butter or margarine
2 tbsps all-purpose flour
2 cups boiling real vegetable broth or water
    plus 2 bouillon cubes
Salt and pepper

Topping
4 slices French bread, cut crosswise
¼ cup shredded yellow cheese
2 tbsps grated Parmesan cheese

---

1. Slice the onions very finely into rings.

2. Melt the butter in a pot, add the onion rings, and sauté over a medium heat until well browned.

3. Mix in the flour and stir well until browned.

4. Add the broth and seasoning, and simmer 30 minutes.

5. Toast the bread on both sides.

6. Combine both types of cheese, and divide between the bread slices. Place under a preheated medium broiler, and toast until golden-brown.

7. Place the slices of bread-and-cheese in the bottom of individual soup bowls or plates and spoon the soup over the top. Serve at once.

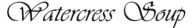

Watercress Soup

SERVES 4

*Watercress makes delicious soup, which can be served hot or cold,
and is packed with vitamins too.*

PREPARATION: 15 mins
COOKING: 45 mins

---

4 tbsps butter
1 leek, cleaned and thinly siced
8 ounces potatoes, peeled and sliced thinly
2¼ cups chicken broth
Pinch grated nutmeg
Salt and freshly ground black pepper
4 big bunches of watercress, washed, trimmed,
    and chopped
3 tbsps half-and-half
Few extra sprigs of watercress, for garnish

---

1. Melt the butter in a large saucepan and gently cook the leek until it is just soft, stirring frequently to prevent it browning.

2. Add the potatoes, stock, nutmeg, and

Step 1 Slowly soften the leek in the melted butter, stirring to prevent it browning.

Step 3 Blend the soup in a food processor or liquidizer until the vegetables are very finely chopped.

seasoning to the saucepan. Bring to the boil, then cover and simmer 15 minutes. Add the watercress, and simmer for a further 10 minutes.

3. Cool the soup slightly, then using a food processor or blender, process until the vegetables are very finely chopped. Rinse the saucepan and stand a fine-meshed nylon sieve over the cleaned pan.

4. Push the soup through the sieve using the back of a wooden spoon, until only the tough stalks remain and the soup in the pan is a fine purée.

5. Adjust the seasoning and stir the cream into the soup. Reheat gently, taking care not to boil it. Serve garnished with the reserved watercress sprigs, and a little extra cream if wished.

Smoked Salmon Bisque

SERVES 6-8

You can buy lox trimmings from supermarkets and delicatessens to use for this soup, if you have no leftovers.

PREPARATION: 10 mins
COOKING: 30 mins

Skin and trimmings of a side of smoked salmon (lox)
1 carrot
1-2 sticks of celery
1 onion, studded with cloves
1 bayleaf
1 tsp salt
Few peppercorns
4 tbsps butter
4 tbsps all-purpose flour
1 tbsp tomato paste
1 wineglass white wine or sherry
4 tbsps light cream and 1 tbsp chopped parsley, for garnishing

1. Put the smoked salmon skin and trimmings in a large saucepan. Coarsely chop the carrot and celery. Add these to the pan along with the onion.

2. Cover with 2½ quarts cold water, add the bayleaf, salt, and peppercorns. Cover the pan and bring to the boil, then simmer 20 minutes.

3. Remove the bayleaf. Take out the onion, remove the cloves, and return the onion to the pan. With a slotted spoon, remove the fish skin and scrape off any remaining flesh, which should also be returned to the pan. Strain half the liquid into a bowl.

4. In another large pan, melt the butter, stir in the flour to make a roux and cook 1 minute. Stir in the tomato paste and gradually add the strained stock, stirring constantly until it thickens. Add the wine or sherry.

5. Put the rest of the broth, containing the fish and vegetables, in a blender and blend for half a minute. Add this to the soup and season if necessary.

6. You can either stir the cream into the soup before serving, or swirl a little on top of each bowl. Garnish with a little chopped parsley.

Indian Tomato Soup

SERVES 4

This highly fragrant and spicy tomato soup makes an interesting appetizer that is also low in calories.

PREPARATION: 15 mins
COOKING: 17-18 mins

---

8 ounces tomatoes
2 tbsps vegetable oil
1 medium-sized onion, chopped
1 green chilli, seeded and finely chopped
3 cloves garlic, crushed
1 tbsp tomato paste
2 cups water or vegetable broth
½ tsp curry powder
Sea salt, to taste
Coriander (cilantro) leaves and green chilies, for garnish

---

1. Cut a small cross in the skin of each tomato and plunge them into boiling water for 30-40 seconds.

2. Remove the tomatoes and carefully peel

Step 2 Remove the tomatoes from the boiling water and carefully peel away the loosened skin.

Step 2 Cut away and discard the hard green core from the tomatoes, and chop the flesh roughly with a sharp knife.

away the loosened skin with a sharp knife. Core and roughly chop the flesh.

3. Heat the oil in a large saucepan and gently sauté the onion, chili, and garlic 3-4 minutes until soft but not browned.

4. Stir in the tomatoes and cook 5 minutes, stirring frequently to prevent the vegetables from burning.

5. Blend the tomato paste with the water and add to the onions and tomatoes. Add the curry powder, season with the salt, and simmer 5-7 minutes.

6. Remove the soup from the heat, and stir in the coriander (cilantro) leaves and the chili halves.

7. Pour the soup into 4-6 serving bowls and serve piping hot. The chili garnish can be discarded before eating.

Sweet Potato Soup

SERVES 4-6

Warm up your winter days with this hearty soup.

PREPARATION: 15 mins
COOKING: 40-55 mins

---

4 tbsps butter or margarine
1 large onion, minced
1 pound sweet potatoes or yams, peeled and diced
2 cups peeled and diced carrots
1 tbsp chopped fresh coriander (cilantro)
Grated zest and juice of 1 lemon
3¾ cups broth
Pepper
Coriander (cilantro) leaves for garnish

---

1. Melt the butter or margarine in a large saucepan, add the onion, and cook until transparent.

2. Add the sweet potato and carrots, and cook over a very low heat 10-15 minutes, stirring occasionally.

3. Add the coriander (cilantro), lemon zest, juice of half the lemon, the broth, and pepper. Cover, and simmer 30-40 minutes.

4. Liquidize the soup in a blender or food processor until almost smooth, but leave some texture to the soup.

5. Return to the pan, and reheat until piping hot. Garnish with coriander (cilantro) leaves and serve immediately.

Wonton Soup

SERVES 6-8

Probably the best-known Chinese soup, this recipe uses ready-made wonton wrappers for ease of preparation.

PREPARATION: 25-30 mins
COOKING: 5-10 mins

---

3 ounces finely ground chicken or lean pork
2 tbsps chopped fresh coriander (cilantro)
3 green onions (scallions), finely chopped
1-inch fresh root ginger, peeled and minced
20-24 wonton wrappers
1 egg, lightly beaten
6¼ cups real chicken broth
1 tbsp dark soy sauce
Dash sesame oil
Salt and pepper
Coriander (cilantro), or watercress, to garnish

---

1. Mix together the chicken or pork, coriander, green onions (scallions), and ginger. Place all the wonton wrappers on a large, flat surface. Brush the edges of the wrappers lightly with beaten egg.

Step 1 Lay the wonton wrappers out on a large surface. Brush the edges with beaten egg.

Step 2 Place a spoonful of filling on half of each wrapper

2. Place a small mound of the meat mixture on each of the wrappers and fold the other half over the top to form a triangle. Press with the fingers to seal the edges well.

3. Bring the stock to the boil in a large saucepan. Add the filled wontons and simmer for 5-10 minutes, or until they float to the surface. Add the remaining ingredients to the soup, using only the coriander (cilantro) or watercress leaves for garnish.

Step 2 Fold over the tops and press firmly with the fingers to seal.

Fennel and Walnut Soup

SERVES 4

A delicious and unusual combination makes this soup perfect for special occasions.

PREPARATION: 15 mins
COOKING: 1 hr

---

1 bulb fennel
1 head celery
1 tbsp olive or sunflower oil
1 large onion, chopped
⅓ cup walnuts, crushed
5 cups vegetable broth, bean broth or water
3 tbsps Pernod or aniseed-flavored liqueur
⅔ cup half-and-half
Salt and pepper
Parsley, to garnish

---

1. Chop the fennel and celery coarsely. Heat the oil over a low heat in a saucepan and sauté the fennel and celery with the onion 20-30 minutes.

2. Add the walnuts and broth, and simmer 30 minutes.

3. Liquidize the simmered ingredients in a blender or food processor, and return to the pot.

4. Add the Pernod, half-and-half, and salt and pepper.

5. Reheat gently without boiling, and serve garnished with chopped parsley.

Hot-and-Sour Soup

SERVES 4-6

This very warming soup is a winter favorite in China. Add the chili sauce and vinegar to suit your taste.

PREPARATION: 25 mins
COOKING: 7-8 mins

2 ounces lean pork
2 ounces peeled, uncooked shrimp
6¼ cups real chicken broth
3 dried Chinese mushrooms, soaked in boiling
    water for 5 minutes, chopped
2 tbsps bamboo shoots, sliced
3 green onions (scallions), shredded
Salt and pepper
1 tbsp sugar
1 tsp dark soy sauce
½ tsp light soy sauce
1-2 tsps chili sauce
1½ tbsps vinegar
Dash sesame oil, and rice wine or sherry
1 egg, well beaten
2 tbsps water mixed with 1 tbsp cornstarch

Step 3 Pour the egg into the hot soup and stir gently to form threads.

1. Trim any remaining fat from the pork and slice it into shreds about 2 inches long and less than ¼ inch thick.

2. Place the pork in a large saucepan with the shrimp and broth. Bring to the boil, then reduce the heat to allow to simmer gently for 4-5 minutes. Add all the remaining ingredients except for the egg and the cornstarch-and-water mixture. Cook a further 1-2 minutes over low heat.

3. Remove the pan from the heat and add the egg gradually, stirring gently until it forms threads in the soup.

4. Mix a spoonful of the hot soup with the cornstarch-and-water mixture and add to the soup, stirring constantly.

5. Bring the soup back to simmering point for 1 minute to thicken the cornstarch. Serve immediately.

Soak the dried mushrooms in boiling water for 5 minutes. Remove with a draining spoon.

Rich Brown Soup

SERVES 4

Use real beef broth as the basis of this soup.

PREPARATION: 30 mins
COOKING: 2 hrs

4 tbsps butter or margarine
5 tbsps all-purpose flour
3¼ cups water
2 cups beef broth
Salt and pepper
Dash Worcestershire sauce
Grated yellow cheese
Fresh parsley, to garnish

1. Heat the butter or margarine in a large pot or soup kettle until melted. Stir in the flour, then cook over a low heat, stirring constantly, until the flour is a rich brown color.

2. Gradually stir in the water and broth. Stir constantly while adding the liquid to prevent lumps forming.

3. Add salt and pepper to taste and Worcestershire sauce. Cover the pot and simmer slowly about 2 hours to fully develop the flavor.

4. Serve sprinkled with grated yellow cheese and garnished with parsley.

Zucchini Soup with Lemon

SERVES 4-6

The fresh taste of lemon and zucchini makes this a delicious soup that can be served either hot or cold.

PREPARATION: 20 mins
COOKING: 25 mins

---

1 medium onion, thinly sliced
2 tbsps olive oil
4 cups trimmed and sliced zucchini
Finely grated rind and juice of 1 large lemon
2 cups chicken broth
Freshly ground black pepper
2 egg yolks
1 cup plain yogurt

---

1. In a large pan, sauté the onion gently in the olive oil 3 minutes until it is just transparent. Add the zucchini and cook a further 2-3 minutes.

2. Stir in all remaining ingredients except the egg yolks and yogurt, cover, and simmer for 20 minutes.

Step 3 Blend the soup in a liquidizer or food processor until it is smooth.

3. Transfer the soup to a liquidizer or food processor, and blend until smooth.

4. Mix the egg yolks into the yogurt and stir into the blended soup. Reheat the soup gently, stirring constantly until it thickens. Do not allow the soup to boil.

5. Serve hot at this stage, or refrigerate until thoroughly chilled.

Step 1 In a large pan, gently sauté the onion until it is just transparent.

Step 4 Mix together the egg yolks and yogurt in a small jug or bowl.

Spicy Chili Bean Soup

SERVES 4-6

This "complete meal" soup is full of flavor, and is ideal for a cold day.

PREPARATION: 30 mins
COOKING: 1 hr

---

3 tbsps vegetable oil
2 onions, coarsely chopped
1 clove garlic, crushed
1 tbsp ground cumin
2 tsps paprika
1 red or green chili, seeded, and finely
   chopped
8 ounces ground beef
3 cups canned tomatoes, chopped
3¾ cups chicken or vegetable broth
3 tbsps tomato paste
1 tsp oregano
1 bayleaf
⅔ cups beer
Freshly ground black pepper
½ cup each of canned red kidney beans,
   chickpeas (garbanzo beans), and white pinto
   beans, drained and thoroughly rinsed

---

1. Heat the oil in a large, heavy-based saucepan. Add the onions and garlic and cook slowly until they become transparent.

2. Stir in the cumin, paprika and chili. Increase

Step 6 Add the drained beans to the soup during the last 15 minutes of cooking time.

the heat and cook quickly 30 seconds, stirring constantly.

3. Add the meat and cook until lightly browned, breaking up any large pieces with a fork.

4. Add the tomatoes and their juice, the broth, tomato paste, oregano, bayleaf, beer, and ground pepper. Stir well, then bring to the boil.

5. Cover and simmer about 50 minutes, checking the level of liquid several times during cooking, and adding more water if needed.

6. During the last 15 minutes of cooking, add the drained beans, stirring them in to mix well.

Turkey Chowder

SERVES 6-8

Serve this good, filling soup with crusty bread for a meal in itself.

PREPARATION: 15 mins
COOKING: 3½ hrs

Turkey bones
1 bayleaf
3 black peppercorns
¼ tsp grated nutmeg
1 onion, unpeeled
1 cup pearl barley, rinsed
3 stalks celery, sliced
3 carrots, diced
1 cup sliced green beans
¾ cup canned sweetcorn, drained
2 tbsps chopped parsley

1. Use the carcass from a roast turkey. Break up the carcass and place in a large pot with any skin and leftover meat, the bayleaf, peppercorns, mace and onion.

2. Pour in 5 quarts cold water to cover the bones, and then cover the pot. Bring to the boil, then simmer, partially covered, about 2 hours.

3. Strain and reserve the broth. Remove any meat from the bones, dice, and reserve.

4. Combine the strained broth, barley, celery, carrots, and green beans. Partially cover and bring to the boil, then reduce the heat and simmer for 1-1½ hrs, or until the barley is tender. Add the corn after about 45 minutes cooking time, and stir in the chopped parsley, and any diced turkey.

Egg-and-Lemon Soup

SERVES 6

This is one of the best-known of all Greek soups. Diced chicken can be added to make it more filling if wished.

PREPARATION: 15 mins
COOKING: 15 mins

6¼ cups real chicken broth
¼ cup Carolina rice, rinsed
2 eggs, separated
Juice of 2 lemons

---

1. Bring the broth to the boil in a large saucepan. When boiling, add the rice, and cook about 10 minutes.

2. Meanwhile, beat the eggs with 1 tbsp cold water about 3 minutes, or until lightly frothy. Add the lemon juice and beat about 1 minute to blend well.

Step 2 Add the lemon juice to the egg yolks, straining out any seeds. Beat for about a minute to blend well.

Step 3 Beat a few spoonfuls of the hot broth into the egg mixture.

3. Beat a few spoonfuls of the hot broth into the egg mixture. Gradually add back to the pan, stirring continuously. Return the soup to the stove and cook on a very low heat about 1-2 minutes, stirring constantly. Do not allow the soup to boil. Serve immediately.

Step 3 Pour the egg mixture back into the broth in a thin, steady stream, stirring continuously. Do not allow to boil.

Wild Rice Soup

SERVES 4

A meal in itself when served with whole bread and a green salad.

PREPARATION: 15 mins
COOKING: 50 mins

¼ cup wild rice
2 cups water
2 onions, chopped
1 tbsp butter or clarified butter
2 sticks celery, chopped
½ tsp dried thyme
½ tsp dried sage
3¾ cups vegetable broth
1 tbsp soy sauce
6 small potatoes, peeled and coarsely chopped
1 carrot, finely diced
Milk or half-and-half

---

1. Add the wild rice to the water, bring to the boil, reduce the heat, and simmer 40-50 minutes or until the rice has puffed and most of the liquid has been absorbed.

2. Meanwhile, in a saucepan, sauté the onions in the butter until transparent. Add the celery, thyme, and sage and cook 5-10 minutes.

3. Add the stock, soy sauce, and potatoes. Simmer about 20 minutes, or until the potatoes are tender.

4. Blend the mixture in a liquidizer until smooth. Return to the pan, add the carrot and wild rice.

5. Add some milk or half-and-half to thin the soup to the desired consistency. Reheat gently, without boiling, and serve.

Lentil Soup with Sausage

SERVES 6-8

This German soup includes bratwurst which helps make this hearty enough for a meal in itself.

PREPARATION: 15 mins, plus 3-4 hrs soaking
COOKING: 1½ hrs

1½ cups brown or red lentils, well washed
4 ounces Canadian bacon, rind removed and
   chopped
1 onion, thinly sliced
4 sticks celery, sliced
2 carrots, peeled and thinly sliced
3 tbsps butter or margarine
3-4 bratwurst, cut into 1-inch pieces
1 tbsp all-purpose flour
1¼ cups water or broth
2 tsps wine vinegar
Salt and pepper

---

1. Soak the lentils in enough water to cover, for 3-4 hours. Drain and place in a large Dutch

Step 1 When lentils have been cooking for about 20 minutes, skim the surface as the soup cooks.

Step 2 Whisk the water or broth into the flour gradually to prevent lumps forming.

oven or soup kettle. Add the bacon, onion, celery, carrots, and 1 quart water. Bring to the boil, cover, and simmer 45 minutes.

2. When lentils are almost cooked, melt the butter in a skillet and fry the bratwurst until brown. Remove and set aside. Stir the flour into the butter in the pan and gradually whisk in the additional water or broth. Bring to the boil, stirring continuously. Add the vinegar and seasonings, and allow to boil about 1 minute.

3. Stir the mixture into the soup, blending thoroughly. Bring back to the boil, then simmer the soup, uncovered, for a further 40-50 minutes, or until the lentils are completely tender. Add the bratwurst and heat through.

Carrot Soup

SERVES 4

Carrots make a most delicious soup that is both filling and quick to prepare.

PREPARATION: 12 mins
COOKING: 25 mins

---

1 pound carrots
1 medium onion
1 medium turnip
2 cloves garlic, crushed
3¼ cups water or vegetable broth
½ tsp dried thyme
½ tsp grated nutmeg
Salt and ground white pepper, to taste
Toasted sunflower seeds, flaked almonds, and
   pistachio nuts, mixed together for garnish

---

1. Peel the carrots and cut them into thick slices. Peel and coarsely chop the onion and turnip.

2. Put the vegetables, garlic, and water or broth, into a large saucepan and bring to the

Step 1 Using a sharp knife, roughly chop the peeled onions and turnip.

boil. Cover the pan, reduce the heat, and simmer 20 minutes.

3. Add the herbs and seasoning, and simmer a further 5 minutes.

4. Using a liquidizer or food processor, blend the soup until it is thick and smooth.

5. Reheat the soup as required, garnishing with the seeds and nuts before serving.

Step 1 Cut the carrots into thick slices, approximately ½-inch thick.

Step 4 Purée the soup in a liquidizer or food processor, until it is thick and smooth.

Split Pea Soup

SERVES 4-6

The ham bone adds lots of flavor to this thick hearty soup.

PREPARATION: 10 minutes, plus overnight
    soaking
COOKING: 1-1¼ hrs

---

2 cups dried split-peas
1 ham bone
1 small onion, minced
1 bayleaf
3 tbsps butter
3 tbsps all-purpose flour
Salt and pepper
1 quart milk
Chopped fresh mint, or other herbs
Croutons

---

1. Soak the peas overnight in enough water to cover. Drain, then place in a large saucepan or Dutch oven with 2½ pints of cold water along with the ham bone, onion, and bayleaf.

2. Bring to the boil, then simmer 45-50 minutes, until the peas are very tender. Remove the ham bone, cut off any meat, and chop it into small pieces.

3. Remove the bayleaf and blend the soup, if wished, then return the meat to the soup.

4. Melt the butter in a large saucepan and stir in the flour until smooth and well blended. Cook 1 minute, add salt and pepper, and gradually stir in the milk.

5. Cook, stirring constantly, until thickened. Add the split-pea mixture, and cook until very thick.

6. Add some chopped mint. Serve with croutons and extra mint.

Index

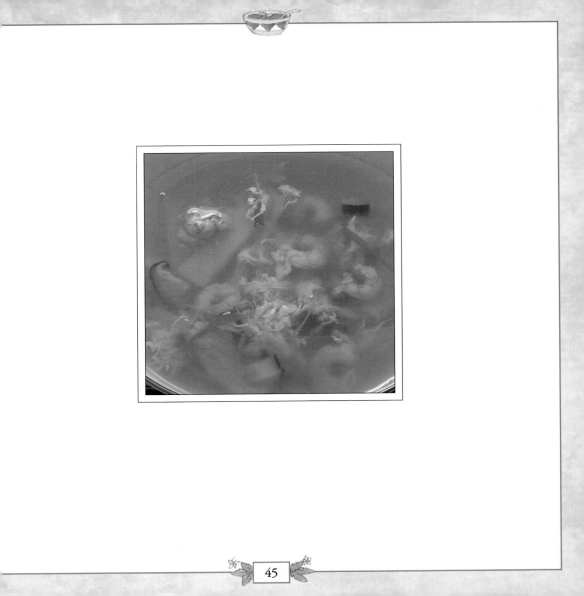